BIGGEST NAMES IN SPORTS
NAOMI OSAKA
TENNIS STAR

by Matt Scheff

Focus Readers
NAVIGATOR

WWW.FOCUSREADERS.COM

Copyright © 2020 by Focus Readers®, Lake Elmo, MN 55042. All rights reserved. No part of this book may be reproduced or utilized in any form or by any means without written permission from the publisher.

Focus Readers is distributed by North Star Editions:
sales@northstareditions.com | 888-417-0195

Produced for Focus Readers by Red Line Editorial.

Photographs ©: Kyodo/AP Images, cover; lev radin/Shutterstock Images, 4–5; Julio Cortez/ AP/Rex Features, 7; Aflo/Rex Features, 9; C.Lotongkum/Shutterstock Images, 10–11; Jacques Brinon/AP Images, 13; Koji Watanabe/Getty Images Sport/Getty Images, 15; Noah Graham/ Getty Images Sport/Getty Images, 16–17; Mai Groves/Shutterstock Images, 19; Rafiq Maqbool/AP Images, 21; Kaname Yoneyama/Yomiuri Shimbun/AP Images, 22–23; Lynne Sladky/AP Images, 25; Mark Schiefelbein/AP Images, 27; Red Line Editorial, 29

Library of Congress Cataloging-in-Publication Data
Library of Congress Cataloging-in-Publication Data is available on the Library of Congress website.

ISBN
978-1-64493-054-0 (hardcover)
978-1-64493-133-2 (paperback)
978-1-64493-291-9 (ebook pdf)
978-1-64493-212-4 (hosted ebook)

Printed in the United States of America
Mankato, MN
012020

ABOUT THE AUTHOR

Matt Scheff is an artist and author living in Alaska. He enjoys mountain climbing, deep-sea fishing, and curling up with his two Siberian huskies to watch tennis.

TABLE OF CONTENTS

CHAPTER 1

Major Stunner 5

CHAPTER 2

From Japan to the United States 11

CHAPTER 3

Going Pro 17

CHAPTER 4

Tennis Superstar 23

At-a-Glance Map • 28
Focus on Naomi Osaka • 30
Glossary • 31
To Learn More • 32
Index • 32

CHAPTER 1

MAJOR STUNNER

Naomi Osaka was just 20 years old when she competed in the 2018 US Open final. It was the first **Grand Slam** final of her career. And she was facing her hero, Serena Williams.

Osaka was ready for the challenge. She blasted one powerful shot after the next. Osaka quickly took control.

Osaka prepares to hit a backhand against Serena Williams during the 2018 US Open final.

She forced Williams to move from side to side. Point by point, Osaka wore down the biggest star in tennis.

Williams had given birth to a baby daughter just 12 months earlier. The birth had required an emergency surgery. Williams also faced several health problems afterwards. As a result,

SERENA WILLIAMS

Serena Williams is Osaka's favorite player. Since Williams turned pro in 1995, she has enjoyed one of the most successful careers in the history of tennis. As of December 2019, she had won a record 23 Grand Slam singles titles. She had also won 14 doubles titles with her sister Venus.

Osaka lunges for a shot during the 2018 US Open.

the crowd at the US Open was cheering hard for Williams. Nearly everyone in the stadium wanted to see her win the match.

7

Osaka won the first **set** 6–2. Williams looked rattled by Osaka's attacking style. In the second set, Osaka built a 5–4 lead. She was one game away from winning her first major title. Osaka served double **match point**. But Williams fought it off. The crowd roared. The fans wanted Williams to make a comeback.

Osaka still had a second match point. She tossed up the ball and blasted a scorching serve. Williams had no chance. Osaka was the champion! She was the first Japanese-born player to win a Grand Slam title.

It should have been the happiest moment of Osaka's career. However, it

Osaka shows off her trophy after winning the 2018 US Open.

was hard to enjoy the victory. The crowd was upset that Williams had lost. Osaka tried to force a smile. But she burst into tears. She had beaten her hero. She also felt guilty that the fans didn't get the ending they had hoped for. It was a **bittersweet** ending to an incredible performance.

CHAPTER 2

FROM JAPAN TO THE UNITED STATES

Naomi Osaka was born on October 16, 1997, in Osaka, Japan. Her mother, Tamaki Osaka, was from Japan. Her father, Leonard François, was from Haiti. The couple met while François was visiting Japan as a student. Naomi was their second child. Their first child, Mari, was 18 months older.

Osaka is home to more than 2.5 million people, making it the third-largest city in Japan.

In 1999, François watched the French Open. American sisters Venus and Serena Williams were the talk of the tournament. François became fixed on the idea that his young daughters would play tennis someday.

When Naomi was three years old, the family moved to a town near New York City. There, the girls had better access to tennis courts.

François began their training. They hit thousands of balls every day. They soon started to play each other. Mari always won. Naomi rarely even won a set. But she was driven by one goal. She wanted to beat her sister.

Venus (left) and Serena Williams celebrate their doubles championship at the 1999 French Open.

Naomi and Mari grew up learning about both Haitian and Japanese culture. The family lived with François's parents, who taught them about Haiti. Meanwhile, their mother taught them about Japan.

13

In 2006, the family moved to a town near Miami, Florida. There, the sisters could practice tennis all year round. They did not attend public school. Instead, they were homeschooled. That gave them extra time to spend on the court. Naomi thrived in Florida. One of her greatest skills was her powerful serve.

MARI OSAKA

Naomi Osaka has become one of the top players in women's tennis. But her sister Mari is also an excellent player. Mari doesn't have the raw power that her younger sister does. Still, she has what it takes to compete at the highest level. In 2018, she rose to her career-best ranking of 280.

Naomi (left) and Mari take part in a doubles match in 2017.

Naomi and Mari had spent most of their lives in the United States. And their father was from Haiti. But when they were ready to turn pro, they decided to represent Japan. That country had few star players in women's tennis. François believed Japan would embrace the girls as soon as they found success.

CHAPTER 3

GOING PRO

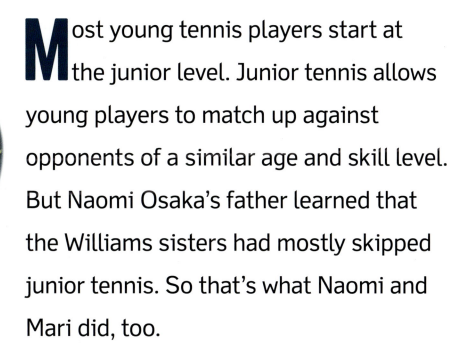

Most young tennis players start at the junior level. Junior tennis allows young players to match up against opponents of a similar age and skill level. But Naomi Osaka's father learned that the Williams sisters had mostly skipped junior tennis. So that's what Naomi and Mari did, too.

A 16-year-old Naomi Osaka plays in the Bank of the West Classic in July 2014.

The Osaka sisters continued to practice until they were old enough to play on the International Tennis Federation (ITF) women's **circuit**. Naomi began playing at ITF events in 2011 when she was 14 years old. Her quickness and power made her a force on the court. Two years later, she turned professional.

In July 2014, Naomi **qualified** for the Women's Tennis Association (WTA) Bank of the West Classic. Her first opponent was Samantha Stosur, a former US Open champion. Naomi quickly showed that she belonged. She attacked Stosur with powerful strokes. She blasted serves that traveled 120 miles per hour (193 km/h).

Naomi stretches for a forehand shot during a 2015 match in Thailand.

Naomi lost the first set. But then she stormed back and won the final two sets. That gave Naomi her first WTA victory. After the match, she said it was the second-biggest victory of her career. The biggest was the first time she beat her sister.

Over the next year, Naomi worked her way up the world rankings. By 2015, she was ranked in the top 250. That was high enough to qualify for Wimbledon and the US Open. Naomi won her first match at the US Open. But she failed to qualify for the **main draw** of either tournament.

Osaka really burst onto the scene in 2016. She qualified for her first Grand Slam main draw at the Australian Open. There she beat Elina Svitolina, who was ranked No. 21 in the world. Osaka eventually lost in the third round of the tournament.

In September 2016, Osaka reached her first WTA final at the Pan Pacific Open.

Osaka returns a serve during the Australian Open in January 2016.

She lost to Caroline Wozniacki, one of the world's best players. But the strong showing lifted Osaka into the top 50 of the rankings. The tennis world took notice. Osaka was named WTA Newcomer of the Year for 2016.

CHAPTER 4

TENNIS SUPERSTAR

Naomi Osaka struggled in 2017. In particular, she had trouble on clay courts. Clay courts tend to slow down the game. The ball bounces higher. It loses much of its speed. However, speed and power are a big part of Osaka's game. As a result, Osaka was at a disadvantage when she played on clay.

Osaka takes part in the French Open, which is played on clay courts.

Even though 2017 was a tough year, it ended on a high note. In Osaka's last tournament of the year, she beat Venus Williams at the Hong Kong Open. Williams was ranked No. 5 in the world.

In 2018, Osaka took the tennis world by storm. It started in January with a strong showing at the Australian Open. There, Osaka beat two top-20 players. She ended up losing to Simona Halep, the world's No. 1 player.

In March, Osaka won the BNP Paribas Open. It was her first professional tournament victory. The highlight came in a rematch with Halep. This time, Osaka won the match in two sets.

Osaka serves to Serena Williams at the 2018 Miami Open.

A week later, at the Miami Open, Osaka faced Serena Williams for the first time. Williams had just returned to tennis after having a baby. Osaka won easily. The two met again in September. This time, Osaka claimed her first Grand Slam title.

By 2019, Osaka was competing for the world's No. 1 ranking. She hoped to claim it at the Australian Open. In the final, Osaka faced Petra Kvitová.

The players exchanged one powerful stroke after another. Kvitová appeared to be in control after winning the second set. But Osaka came back strong in the third. On match point, Osaka blasted a

BIG IN JAPAN

Japan has not had much success in women's tennis. In fact, Osaka was the first Japanese-born woman to hold the world's top ranking. Her quick rise has made her a huge star in Japan. Fans love her raw power as well as her calm, quiet personality.

Osaka shouts for joy after winning a set at the 2019 Australian Open.

powerful serve. Kvitová's return sailed out of bounds, giving Osaka the victory.

Osaka's celebration was on. She had just won her second straight Grand Slam title. She had also claimed the world's No. 1 ranking. Her amazing climb to the top of the tennis world was complete.

AT-A-GLANCE MAP

NAOMI OSAKA

- Height: 5 feet 11 inches (180 cm)
- Weight: 152 pounds (69 kg)
- Birth date: October 16, 1997
- Birthplace: Osaka, Japan
- High school: Broward Virtual School (homeschooled)
- Major awards: WTA Newcomer of the Year (2016); US Open Champion (2018); Australian Open Champion (2019); WTA No. 1 Ranking (2019)

FOCUS ON
NAOMI OSAKA

Write your answers on a separate piece of paper.

1. Write a paragraph summarizing the main ideas of Chapter 2.

2. Osaka represents Japan, but she has lived most of her life in the United States. Do you agree with her decision to represent Japan? Why or why not?

3. Who did Osaka beat in the finals to win the 2018 US Open?
- **A.** Venus Williams
- **B.** Serena Williams
- **C.** Petra Kvitová

4. Tennis experts believe the French Open may be the most difficult Grand Slam event for Osaka to win. What might explain that belief?
- **A.** Osaka does not speak French.
- **B.** The French Open is played on clay courts.
- **C.** No Japanese player has ever won the French Open.

Answer key on page 32.

GLOSSARY

bittersweet
Involving a mixture of happiness and sadness.

circuit
A series of tournaments that professional tennis players take part in.

Grand Slam
One of the four major tennis events. They include the Australian Open, the French Open, Wimbledon, and the US Open.

main draw
The part of a tournament when players are in an elimination bracket.

match point
A point that could end a tennis match.

qualified
Played well enough to take part in a tournament.

set
Part of a tennis match. To win a set, a player must win six games.

TO LEARN MORE

BOOKS

Fishman, Jon M. *Serena Williams*. Minneapolis: Lerner Publications, 2017.

Gitlin, Marty. *The Best Tennis Players of All Time*. Minneapolis: Abdo Publishing, 2015.

Labrecque, Ellen. *Top 10 Women Athletes*. Mankato, MN: The Child's World, 2018.

NOTE TO EDUCATORS

Visit **www.focusreaders.com** to find lesson plans, activities, links, and other resources related to this title.

INDEX

Australian Open, 20, 24, 26

French Open, 12

Haiti, 11, 13, 15
Halep, Simona, 24

International Tennis Federation (ITF), 18

Japan, 8, 11, 13, 15, 26

Kvitová, Petra, 26–27

Miami, Florida, 14

New York City, 12

Osaka, Mari, 11–15, 17

Stosur, Samantha, 18
Svitolina, Elina, 20

US Open, 5, 7, 18, 20

Williams, Serena, 5–9, 12, 17, 25
Williams, Venus, 6, 12, 17, 24
Wimbledon, 20
Women's Tennis Association (WTA), 18–21
Wozniacki, Caroline, 21

Answer Key: 1. Answers will vary; **2.** Answers will vary; **3.** B; **4.** B